Contents

About the author

Richard Cresswell has worked in social care for 19 years. He has worked in many areas of health and social care including learning disability and mental health. Richard has worked as a support worker, deputy manager and home manager of various learning disability charities and trusts. Since 2003 he has worked for the London Borough of Tower Hamlets as a trainer, NVQ assessor, and internal verifier on various health and social care awards, including the learning disability award framework and qualifications, the Registered Manager's Award, and the Leadership and Management for Care Services NVQ. Richard also works for Lifetime Awarding as an EQAC on health and social care qualifications. He has previously co-written the *GCSE Health and Social Care* textbook for Folens, and learning disability optional units for OCR.

Acknowledgements

Thank you to all my colleagues at the London Borough of Tower Hamlets Work Based Learning Service (HSC team): Jenny Dutton, Jackie Tillyard, Sharon Bissette-Campbell, Cheryl Heath and Sajna Begum. Thanks also to Joe Prendiville from The Hub and Jane Eley from Lewisham College for giving me the knowledge and inspiration to plan the sessions and learning activities contained in them.

Introduction

Care quality guides

Pavilion's care quality guides aim to help you refresh, develop or extend your learning in key areas of practice.

- If you are new to working with a particular client group or in a new role, you can use the material to quickly develop knowledge you will need, and where appropriate, work towards a relevant qualification.
- If you are a more experienced worker, you can use the guides to refresh your learning and to contribute towards your continuing professional development.
- If you are a manager, you can use these guides with staff to meet your responsibilities for providing induction and staff supervision, and opportunities for training and development. This will contribute towards meeting Care Quality Commission (CQC) standards.

Supervision and Continuing Professional Development (CPD)

This guide can be used for continuing professional development. If you are a manager, you might like to ask your staff members to work through it section by section, completing the thinking activities and practice activities each contains. Their responses can be discussed as part of ongoing supervision, and on completion of the guide, you can both fill in the CPD certificate at the end.

This guide, and the activities it contains, will take approximately 12 hours to work through.

Meeting the Care Quality Commission (CQC) standards

If you are a manager or provider of a health and social care service, you can use this guide for induction and staff development in order to contribute towards meeting Government standards and to prepare for quality checks and inspections. In particular, using this guide with your staff will contribute towards ensuring that they have training and CPD opportunities to strengthen and develop their skills and knowledge.

Qualifications Credit Framework (QCF)

This guide provides underpinning knowledge for unit LD 202: Support person-centred thinking and planning, and the thinking and practice activities can contribute to evidence of learning. The following table maps the content to the QCF learning outcomes.

NB Pavilion also publishes a QCF workbook that covers all the learning outcomes and includes assessment questions and evidence log. There is an accompanying training pack which can be used by managers and trainers for QCF training or for CPD (Full information at www.pavppub.com).

How the content of this guide maps to the QCF unit LD 202: Support person-centred thinking and planning

Content of guide	LD 202 Learning outcome (LO)
Section 1 The principles and practice of person-centred thinking, planning and reviews	**LO1** Understand the principles and practice of person-centred thinking, planning and reviews
Section 2 The context within which person-centred thinking and planning takes place	**LO2** Understand the context within which person-centred thinking and planning takes place
Section 3 Your role in person-centred planning, thinking and reviews	**LO3** Understand own role in person-centred planning, thinking and reviews
Section 4 Applying person-centred thinking in relation to your own life	**LO4** Be able to apply person-centred thinking in relation to own life
Section 5 Implementing person-centred thinking and person-centred reviews	**LO5** Be able to implement person-centred thinking and person-centred reviews

Section 1

The principles and practice of person-centred thinking, planning and reviews

Introduction

This section looks at the nine core values that you will need to practise and think about in order to support an individual in person-centred thinking and planning. It defines person-centred thinking, planning and reviews, and explores the difference this approach can make to individuals with learning disabilities and their families. The section also introduces some person-centred planning tools and describes the person-centred review process.

The beliefs and values on which person-centred thinking and planning is based

When thinking about person-centred planning it is vital to promote the values and beliefs of service users. The following nine person-centred values should be at the heart of everything that you do when planning and thinking with the people you work with: individuality, rights, choice, privacy, independence, dignity, respect, partnership and equal opportunities. We are now going to look at each of these in a little more detail.

Individuality

Try to find out what the person you are supporting likes and dislikes. This could be simple things like what they want to eat and where they want to go and spend their spare time. It is important to make sure that every service user that you work with is allowed to express themselves, their hopes and dreams, interests and needs, and their own personality, through everything that they do.

Rights

Every one of the people that you work with has rights. These are emphasised in the Human Rights Act (1998). Just because somebody has a learning disability and may not always be able to make decisions in the same way that we do, or at the same speed that we do, it does not mean that they cannot enjoy the 16 basic human rights laid down in the act. It is important that service users are given access to an advocate. An advocate is someone who speaks up for someone on their behalf if they are not able to do so without help. Another act of parliament that governs rights is the Equality Act (2010) (replacing acts such as the Disability Discrimination Act (1995) and the Sex Discrimination Act (1975)).

Key learning point

You cannot make plans with someone without looking at each of these nine core values.

Choice

It is natural for us to make a lot of choices in our everyday life. This could be choosing the food we eat, through to who we want to live with and how we want to live our lives in general. People with learning disabilities aren't always given access to choice as much as they should be. It is extremely important to make sure that the people you work with are given choice and if person-centred thinking and planning are in place, this should not be a problem. We also need to consider how choice will be given to someone who has a severe or profound learning disability, where establishing choice may be quite difficult. It is therefore necessary to work with a variety of different professionals, such as psychologists, learning disability nurses, speech and language therapists, and family members and friends in order to establish good practice when giving choice to people.

Privacy

We all need privacy in our lives. This may be for things such as going to the toilet, having a bath or shower, or just when we need some quiet time on our own in our bedrooms or our living areas. Obtaining privacy can be quite easy for us, but a person with a learning disability may be living with other people in a group or shared home. Try to find a way of providing people with their own space and encouraging people to take time out if they need to. Always knock on someone's bedroom door before entering and make sure you wait to be asked to come in.

Independence

Most people enjoy doing things for themselves. It gives them a sense of achievement and ensures that they develop new life skills. Of course, none of us are really completely independent and we all need help at some point in our lives. This may be in the form of moral support from our friends and family or physical support, such as someone helping us to go on a journey. Make sure that you find out what level of support the person needs in order to complete a task. This should be done as part of the person-centred planning process and the right level of support should be planned for. If an individual is given too much independence in a task, they may fail and this could be psychologically upsetting for them and possibly even dangerous. If they are given too little independence in a task, they are likely to become more dependent on the support that you give and lose skills that they already possess. It is vital that you empower the person by giving them the right information and the correct level of support to feel worthy and able to develop as human beings.

Dignity

Everybody needs to be treated in a dignified way. People with learning disabilities have the same right to dignity as anyone else in society. We should never treat the people that we support in an undignified, inhumane

Thinking activity

How might people who work with people with learning disabilities fail to respect these nine core values?

and degrading way, for example, helping someone have a bath and then taking them back to their room without putting a dressing gown on them, therefore allowing them to be exposed to other people they live with, with no clothes on. Other inhumane treatment could be not helping someone to change an incontinence pad on a regular basis and therefore leaving them in soiled clothing. Equally as important is trying to advise the individual when they want to do something that would embarrass them or make them look foolish. Do not feel that this is a bad thing. If you have the service user's best interests at heart it is good practice to ensure that they understand any consequences of their actions.

Respect

It is important to demonstrate respect towards the people you work with through your actions. This could include the way that you talk to them and the tone of your voice. This could also be demonstrated by how much interest you take in what they do, such as work they have done or something they have made at a day centre. If you do not show respect towards the individual, how can you expect them to respect you and the things that you say to them?

Partnership

A big part of the role that you play with people with learning disabilities is based on partnership between the person that you support and others. This includes you as the worker and the individual's key worker, family and friends, doctors and nurses, speech and language therapists, psychologists, occupational therapists, case managers and social workers and other people, such as the service manager and support workers. Without a partnership between the service user and all of these people there would be no effective person-centred plans in place. Everyone needs to work together as a team on behalf of, and in partnership with, the individual who is at the centre of the whole process.

Equal opportunities

People with learning disabilities are often discriminated against in society either directly or indirectly. Under the Human Rights Act (1998) and

Thinking activity

Have you ever attended a review where the person with a learning disability has had little or no input into the planning or review?

Why do you think that was?

the Equality Act (2010) all people with learning disabilities enjoy the same social status as people who do not have learning disabilities. The General Social Care Council (now the Health and Care Professions Council) laid down guidelines in 2010 stating that all social care workers need to:

- protect the rights and promote the interests of service users and carers
- strive to establish and maintain the trust and confidence of service users and carers
- promote the independence of service users, while protecting them as far from possible from danger and harm
- respect the rights of service users, while seeking to ensure that their behaviour does not harm themselves or other people.

If you work within the nine values described here, you are probably thinking in a person-centred way.

Defining person-centred practice

Person-centred planning

This has been developed as a way of supporting people with learning disabilities to have maximum control over the way that they plan their own care. It uses a collection of tools and approaches that give people with learning disabilities and those who support them simple ways of planning effective care. Person-centred planning should be based around the nine core values listed earlier in the section. There are a number of different tools that can be used including: MAPS, PATH, personal futures planning, one page profiles, essential lifestyle planning and hospital passports (see pages 9–10).

Key learning points

The planning and review must place the person at the centre of all that happens.

Effective person-centred planning and review helps people to develop skills for life, forever.

Person-centred reviews

These meetings are held with the service user and others who are central to the care provided. They are used to review the person-centred plan. As a key worker you may wish to support the service user to invite the people who make a difference in their lives to the meeting. Together you can help them to produce a person-centred plan that will allow them to develop, flourish and realise their dreams.

The difference that person-centred thinking can make to individuals and their families

A person-centred plan is a working and live document. This plan should not live in a locked drawer at the bottom of a filing cabinet gathering dust! It should be shared with those who work with the person being supported, but always with their permission. There is no point in creating a super document that everyone has been involved in and then not sharing it with everyone who is supporting the service user.

Good person-centred thinking and planning can make all the difference to a service user's life. It can provide them with opportunities that they would not have otherwise had, and allow them to realise their dreams and aspirations. If the service user has an innovative and knowledgeable person supporting them then they can flourish and develop new skills. Good person-centred thinking and planning can allow people who did not have skills in the past to develop them and live fuller lives. It can minimise problems such as behaviour that challenges. It is important to get people with different knowledge and expertise involved so these can be used to help the person develop.

Person-centred thinking tools

Here are some examples of different person-centred thinking tools.

PATH

PATH deals with an individual's ideal future or dream and how to move closer to it. It looks at how the service user can plan direct action in order to achieve their dream. For a good explanation of PATH see www.edg-sco.org/index.html?pid=112 or the Inclusion Press guide, *PATH: Planning possible positive futures* (Pearpoint *et al*, 1993).

Hospital passports

These are important plans used on a short-term basis while a person is in hospital. A passport allows doctors and nurses and other hospital staff to provide care and support to the person, and allows them to experience as little distress as is humanly possible in such a difficult situation. For a good example of a hospital passport see www.surreyhealthaction.org/downloads/hospital%20passport%20surrey.pdf.

Personal futures planning

This involves a group of committed people who describe a person's life now and look at what they would like to do in the future. This allows people

Thinking activity

What is important to the people that you work with?

How do you enable them to achieve their goals and what difference does that make to their lives?

Key learning points

Different planning tools work best for different people. You need to help the individual choose the best one(s) for them.

One page profiles are a snapshot of the individual that you work with. They should be easy for people to read and digest in a short amount of time.

to learn more about the individual's life and create a vision for their future. For more information see http://edg.usablewebsites.org/files/Personal_Futures_Planning.pdf.

Essential lifestyle planning

This is a detailed planning tool and looks at how a person's life is now and how it could be improved in the future. It allows people to find out what is important to that person and what support they need in place to have a good quality of life. For more information see www.nwtdt.com/Archive/pcp/1dayoverview.pdf.

MAPS

This is a tool that focuses on gathering information for planning based on the history of the person. This can be used with individuals and their teams and organisations. The process should be facilitated by professionals who understand the stages of the planning process. For information about MAPS see www.edg-sco.org/index.html?pid=112.

Living descriptions

This tool helps someone find out what is important to them in their everyday lives and can develop from a one page profile (see page 11). It is a useful tool to use when people receive paid support as it helps staff to provide support in a way that works for that person.

One page profiles

A one page profile is a planning tool that focuses on what is important to an individual. It may include what others like and admire about that person and what is important to that person in their lives. It will give people ideas about how to support the person on

Thinking activity

What are the different tools that you have used in order to help people plan and develop?

Make a list and consider which ones worked best and why.

Example of a one page profile

Name: *Steve*

What others like and admire about me:

I am caring and sensitive to other people's feelings

I am good at using computers

I know lots about films

I am a good friend

I like to help by making hot drinks for people

What is important to me:

My family

Watching films

Going to football matches

Avoiding loud noises

Meeting my friends for a chat

How to support me:

Support me to manage my money

Help me to eat a healthy diet and stay active

Remind me to take my medication

Listen to me and help me to tell others how I am feeling

What is important to me for the future:

Getting a job

Being able to go on holiday with my friends

Attending important family events

Completed by: *Jim – key worker*

a daily basis and what is important to them in their future – the dreams that they would like to realise. It is usually a one page document that is easy and quick to read. It is thus ideal for busy members of staff, new members of staff or agency staff who can quickly read it and digest the information in it.

Thinking activity

What is the most important information that you would include in a one page profile for one of the people you support?

Why is it important for people to know this information?

The person-centred review process

When conducting the person-centred review process it is important to invite all those professionals who are key to the person's life. This includes members of the multidisciplinary team, such as psychologists and speech therapists. The review process should be set up in an organised fashion. The key worker should always meet with the service user first and plan what they would like to talk about and implement as a result of their review. Equally, you should find out who the person wants to invite to their review and when they would like to have it. The service user should be given plenty of time to prepare and those attending should be given plenty of notice. Nobody should be attending the review unless they are invited and unless the service wants them there, even if they are a family member. The review should be clearly recorded and the correct person-centred planning tool should be used to record the outcome. Nothing should be put into the review that was not decided at the meeting, and the person involved should be at the centre of this review process at all times. There should be no surprises for the service user and the results of the review should be shared with the core staff team, once permission has been given by the service user themself.

Thinking activity

Why is it important to thoroughly prepare for the person-centred review process?

What could happen if this is not done?

Summary

The first learning outcome has looked at the key values underpinning person-centred thinking and planning, and how we should foster these values whenever we plan and review with service users. We have looked at the people who may be involved in this process and the different types of person-centred planning tools that are available.

Key learning point

The review process enables us to review the effectiveness of planning and should involve members of the wider multidisciplinary team.

Practice activity 1

Think about a review you have attended.

What steps did you or the person organising the review have to go through to make sure that the review was person-centred?

Section 2

The context within which person-centred thinking and planning takes place

Introduction

This section focuses on the current legislation, policy and guidance that underpins person-centred thinking and planning. We will look at important legislation and policy such as the Mental Capacity Act (2005), the Equality Act (2010), *Valuing People* (2001), *Valuing People Now* (2009), the Human Rights Act (1998) and personalisation in social services. We will also look at the way person-centred thinking and planning should be used in teams and with the individuals you work with.

Current legislation, policy and guidance underpinning person-centred thinking and planning

It is important to consider the following legislation in person-centred thinking and planning with the people that you work with.

The Mental Capacity Act (2005)

There are five key principles in the act:

- Every adult has the right to make their own decisions and must be assumed to have capacity to make them unless it is proved otherwise.
- A person must be given all practicable help before anyone treats them as unable to make their own decisions.
- Just because an individual makes what may be seen as an unwise decision, they should not be treated as lacking capacity to make that decision.
- Anything done or any decision made on behalf of a person who lacks capacity must be done in their best interests.
- Anything done for or on behalf of a person who lacks capacity should be the least restrictive of their basic rights and freedoms.

Valuing People (2001) and *Valuing People Now* (2009)

The key messages in *Valuing People*:

- People with learning disabilities should have the same rights and choices as everyone else.
- People with learning disabilities have the right to be treated with dignity and respect.
- People with learning disabilities should have the same chances and responsibilities as everyone else.
- Family carers and families of people with learning disabilities have the right to the same hopes and choices as other families.

The Equality Act (2010)

The Equality Act (2010) strengthens the law in important ways to help tackle discrimination and inequality. For individuals with learning disabilities and those who support them, it introduces some important changes:

- it protects a person from being discriminated against because they are linked or associated with an individual with disabilities, making it unlawful for a business or service provider to discriminate against a family member because they are associated with an individual with learning disabilities
- direct discrimination against people with disabilities is now unlawful when individuals are accessing goods and services as well as in the workplace

- it is unlawful to discriminate against an individual because of something connected with their disability (so-called 'discrimination arising from disability')
- it is unlawful to cause indirect discrimination; this is when there is a rule, policy or practice that is for everyone but that makes things harder for people with a disability – for example, children with disabilities not being able to go to the toilet at school because of a ban on teachers lifting heavy objects, which includes children
- disability harassment is unlawful; this is when someone's behaviour violates the dignity of a person with a disability or creates an environment for them that is intimidating, hostile, degrading, humiliating or offensive.

It is too early to tell how effective the act will be in improving the day-to-day experiences of individuals with learning disabilities and their families. Much will depend on how the legislation s used and applied in the courtroom. However, it is clear that the act has improved legal protection against discrimination for these individuals and over time this should translate into increased equality and social inclusion.

Key learning points

Key legislation means we must provide the service users we support with effective planning and review processes.

Personalisation aims to put the person at the centre of getting the services they need.

The Human Rights Act (1998)

This includes giving everyone the human right to:

- life
- liberty
- respect for private and family life
- freedom of thought, conscience and religion, and freedom to express your beliefs
- freedom of expression

Thinking activity

Think about countries that do not have a Human Rights Act and how it affects those people who live there.

How do you think that this legislation helps us in our daily lives?

- freedom of assembly and association
- marry and to start a family
- not be discriminated against in respect of these rights and freedoms
- an education.

The relationship between person-centred planning and personalised services

When using person-centred thinking, planning and review you should make sure that you are aware of the personalisation agenda.

Personalisation means:

- tailoring support to people's individual needs
- ensuring that people have access to information, advocacy and advice to make informed decisions about their care and support
- finding new collaborative ways of working (sometimes known as co-production) that support people to actively engage in the design, delivery and evaluation of services
- developing local partnerships to co-produce a range of services for people to choose from and opportunities for social inclusion and community development
- developing the right leadership and organisational systems to enable staff to work in creative, person-centred ways
- embedding early intervention, re-ablement and prevention so that people are supported early on and in a way that is right for them
- recognising and supporting carers in their role, while enabling them to maintain a life beyond their caring responsibilities
- ensuring that all citizens have access to universal community services and resources – a total system response.

Ways that person-centred thinking can be used in teams

When using person-centred thinking and planning in teams, you should be meeting as a team on a regular basis.

Thinking activity

Why is personalisation important to the people that we work with?

How do you think that it provides them with greater choice in their daily lives?

To work as effectively as possible, you might also find it helpful to consider who plays what 'role' with your team. Belbin (2011) identified nine roles, each making different contributions to team playing.

It is important to try out new ways of working and different styles of person planning templates. Think about having an away day where you all get together and try thought-showering ideas around different ways of planning and thinking. Look at different scenarios around person-centred thinking and planning, such as what you would do if the person could not communicate their feelings and thoughts to you, or if the person had family members that were difficult to deal with. This will not only improve your planning and thinking skills, it will improve morale and relationships within your team and can be used as a continuous professional development activity. Doing these sorts of exercises will improve your person-centred thinking and planning and benefit the service users that you support.

Key learning point

There is no 'I' in team! Teams need to work together to make person-centred thinking, planning and review happen.

Summary

This section has briefly covered the Equality Act (2010), the Mental Capacity Act (2005), *Valuing People* and *Valuing People Now* (DH, 2001 & 2009) and the Human Rights Act (1998), and outlined how these should link into your person-centred thinking and planning with the people that you work with. You should have also learned about what personalisation is and how it links into person-centred planning and thinking.

Thinking activity

Research Belbin's team roles (2011) and look at how they apply to the team that you work in.

What role(s) do you think you play in your team?

Practice activity 2

How does your team use person-centred thinking and planning to move forward in its goals?

Section 3

Your role in person-centred planning, thinking and reviews

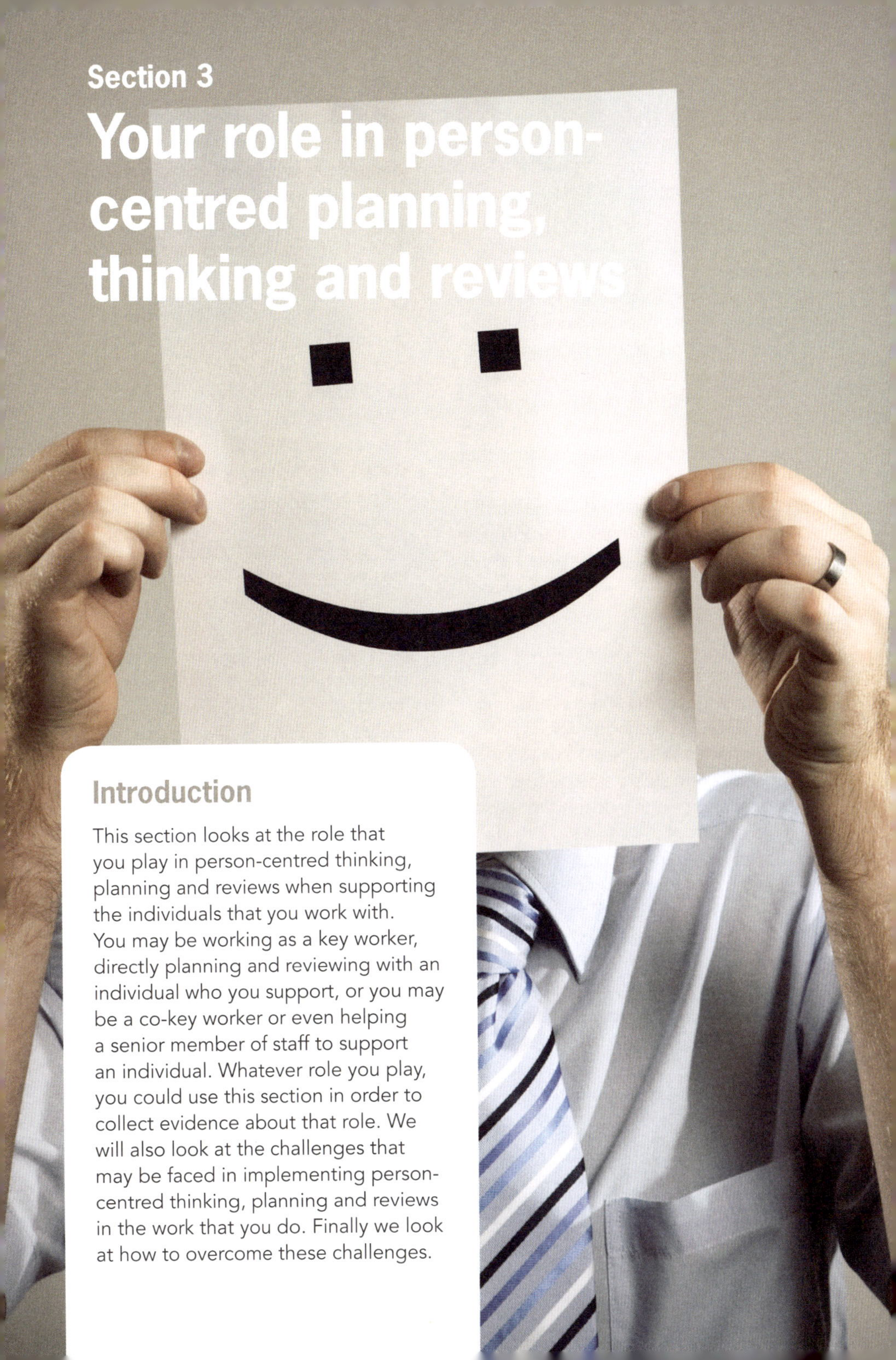

Introduction

This section looks at the role that you play in person-centred thinking, planning and reviews when supporting the individuals that you work with. You may be working as a key worker, directly planning and reviewing with an individual who you support, or you may be a co-key worker or even helping a senior member of staff to support an individual. Whatever role you play, you could use this section in order to collect evidence about that role. We will also look at the challenges that may be faced in implementing person-centred thinking, planning and reviews in the work that you do. Finally we look at how to overcome these challenges.

Your role in person-centred thinking, planning and reviews when supporting individuals

Empathy is a major part of the person-centred thinking, planning and review process. As someone who works in social care you should be aware of the person-centred values that were discussed in the first section of this guide. You should be aware of how to apply them to yourself and those that you work with. How would you feel if you were not consulted about what you want to do with your life and how you want to live out your dreams and aspirations? You would probably feel very powerless.

Your role is very important in the person-centred thinking, planning and review process when supporting individuals. As someone who is supporting and helping to write a person-centred plan, you need to understand that this document forms a major part of the service user's life in terms of what they do, how they do it and how they are supported. You may not be a key worker and may not write the plan directly, but it is role to make sure that you and others follow what has been decided in the person-centred plan. You should make sure that people are aware of the plan and the most important things they should concentrate on. You should be aware of how to do this, whether or not you are the key worker who writes the plan.

If you are responsible for helping the person to write their person-centred plan, then you need to be aware of key factors. These could include: their likes and dislikes; hopes, dreams and aspirations; personal care needs; dietary needs; family and friends; medical history and any illnesses. You should also consider any other areas that are important to the service user that you work with. You will also need to consult with experts who can advise the service user and yourself on the best way to meet the needs of the person concerned. It may also be your job to arrange the reviews and invite the people that the service user needs or wants to attend.

Thinking activity

Who would you most like to support you if you needed help to write your person-centred plan?

Why is this?

Practice activity 3

You may or may not act as a key worker for one of the individuals that you support. You will, however, play an important role in supporting the individuals that you work with and collecting vital information in the form of written records and reporting at team meetings and briefings.

Describe your role in person-centred thinking, planning and reviews when supporting the individuals that you work with.

Identifying challenges that may be faced in implementing person-centred approaches

Thinking activity

Are there any obstacles that stand in the way of you and your dreams?

If so, who or what are they?

How will you deal with these obstacles?

Many sorts of challenges may arise as a result of the person-centred planning and review process. Person-centred planning is never easy, as it deals with real human beings who may have a variety of different issues. It is important to all strive to overcome challenges in the person-centred planning and review process. You may have already encountered problems implementing the person-centred planning and review process, including: over-protective families and friends who feel activities may be inappropriate or too dangerous for the person that you support to be involved with; anxiety of the person who you work with in certain situations or places which may make them unwelcome in certain activities.

More often than not, there may be problems with funding and raising money in order to pay for activities that the service user you are supporting may wish to be involved in. There may also be health and safety risks to the service user, which outweigh the benefit of the activity and make it too dangerous for them. Maybe a service user has problems with their health, which makes it hazardous for them to become involved in an activity. For example, photosensitive epilepsy may be aggravated by a service user going to a nightclub, and diabetes may prevent service users from indulging in rich puddings and sugary foods.

Other challenges may include poor staffing in a project where people live and work, which means that there are problems in supporting service users to access activities.

How can we overcome these challenges?

Implementing the person-centred thinking, planning and review process is never an easy task. You are dealing with real people who have real emotions and feelings and sometimes quite profound learning disabilities.

You may also be dealing with families who are over-protective and services that are overstretched and under-resourced. It is important for you to be tenacious in your approach at all times. You will not get much done if you fail at first and then give up. Make sure that you try different approaches and if one fails, try something different. You need to consider: if you were doing something for yourself and one thing did not work, would you just give up? It is important for you to think of new and innovative ways in which to help individuals access services if you feel it is to their advantage.

You will find many challenges in the person-centred planning process and it is important to ensure that you get as many professional people involved as possible to help you and the service user realise their dreams and aspirations.

Key learning point

It is important that people who are helping to create plans are good at problem-solving and do not easily give up when faced with challenges.

Summary

This section has focused on helping you to identify the role you play in person-centred thinking, planning and review. You should be able to identify challenges from your own practice and that of others in person-centred planning and review. You should also be able to identify ways in which to overcome the difficulties in implementing person-centred planning, thinking and review.

Practice activity 4

When implementing person-centred thinking, planning and reviews in your own work, you may often come across challenges.

Identify some of these challenges and how you can overcome them.

Section 4

Applying person-centred thinking in relation to your own life

Introduction

This section asks you to put yourself in the shoes of someone who is developing their own person-centred planning and review. It is important for you to be able to empathise with somebody who is having their own planning and review carried out. For this reason, you will be asked to consider how to use a person-centred thinking tool in relation to your own life and identify what is working and what is not. You will be asked to think about identifying and recording your own relationship circles. You will need to be able to identify how helpful the person-centred thinking tool was and then you'll need to prepare for your own person-centred review!

Using a person-centred thinking tool in relation to your own life to identify what is working and not working

To be able to use a person-centred thinking tool in relation to the life of the person you are supporting, it is important for you to be able to use one in relation to your own life. Think about the things that you like to do and the ways that you like to do them. Think about the things that you like, such as music and films. Think about the foods you like to eat, the restaurants you like to eat in, the places you like to go to and your favourite activities. Look at the things that you would like to achieve in your life and how you would go about achieving them. Do you have any aspirations and dreams, maybe to own a racing car or to climb Mount Everest? The fact is that everyone is allowed to dream, so it is important to be able to help the person you support to have their dreams, even if they won't or can't come true. When planning your person-centred plan and review how would you do it? Who would you invite? Where would you hold your review? These are all things to consider when writing your own person-centred plan. Think about the things that really annoy you and the types of behaviour that you would not expect from the staff that support you. This may give you an insight into what it's like to need a plan in order to be supported to live a normal life.

Key learning point

Writing a plan that meets your own support needs will give you insight into how to prepare plans for others.

Describing your own relationship circle

In order for you to plan your own review, it is important to establish what your relationship circle is. Your relationship circle consists of the things, places and people that are important to you. This could be the

Thinking activity

What could happen to the people that you support if they did not have effective plans in place?

Practice activity 5

Complete your own one page profile using this profile sheet template.

One page profile

Name:

What others like and admire about me:

What is important to me:

How to support me:

What is important to me for the future:

Did it make you think about what was working in your life and what may not be working quite as well?

school you went to or the college you attended, or the place that you work and the people that support you in that place of work. Look at where you live and who you live with. Do you have a partner and children or do other people live with you, such as flatmates? There are many people and places that are important to you and your life and without them your options would be limited, especially if you were a person with learning disabilities who relied on these people for support.

Key learning point

A relationship circle is an essential part of the planning and review process.

Reviewing your plan

When working with person-centred thinking and planning tools it is important to review the processes that you have been through and what you found useful and not so useful. Reviewing a plan helps you to improve the process for next time and helps you think of better ways to plan for services. Better planning may include the services that you access and how you access them, such as making sure that services are within an easy travelling distance from your own home or that you have access to disabled facilities etc. You need to think about what is important to you and how the tool that you use has helped you to plan actions in your own life. It is important to make sure that you choose the right plan for you and you may need to consider whether you use MAPS or PATH (see pages 9–10). Perhaps you need to spend a short period of time in hospital and a hospital passport may be necessary. Whatever you choose, you need to be at the centre of this person-centred process at all times, and decisions being made should be all about you, what you want and what is best for you. Going through this process should help you understand what the process is

Thinking activity

Why is it important to have a relationship circle?

What could happen if you did not have one?

Practice activity 6

Use the relationship circle diagram below to list your significant relationships.

Write down the impact that each of these people has on your life – positively or negatively – and how they help you to realise your dreams and aspirations.

The relationship circle

List your key relationships under each heading.

Name:

Family

Friends

Work/school/ day centre

Home and other paid support

like for the people you support who really do rely on having good person-centred plans in place.

Thinking about the review process is extremely important as this will help you to be able to plan how best to meet people's changing needs. There is no point in having a plan in place if it does not change as people's needs change. A plan should be reviewed on a regular basis and should involve all of those people that are integral to

Thinking activity

Why do we have person-centred plans and reviews?

What could happen if the review process did not take place?

Practice activity 7

Looking back at practice activities 5 and 6, how useful do you think completing these two exercises was?

Did they help to frame any problems you are currently experiencing?

its function. These will be people such as the service user themselves, yourself, and other members of the multidisciplinary team as we have previously discussed. Think about how you would prepare your own review: what sort of information would you like people to know about you? What sort of things do you enjoy doing and want to do in the future? What are your dreams and aspirations, your likes and dislikes? Think about the support that you need to carry out daily tasks and activities. Will that support always be the same or will you require more or less support in the future? Do you need transport or somebody to accompany you? The following factors are also important things to consider when planning for your review process:

- Who do you want to support you in your review?
- Who do you want to invite to your review?
- Is there anybody you really do not want at your review?
- When do you want to hold your review and where do you want to hold it?

Key learning points

Reviewing a plan will allow for developments to take place and should also introduce improvements in the process.

The service user must be at the centre of everything that happens in the review process. They must be consulted in all aspects of it.

Summary

In this section you have developed your understanding about how the person-centred planning and review process works by applying it to yourself. You have been given the chance to think about your own one page profile or similar person-centred planning tool, to describe your own relationship circle, review the person-centred thinking tool and prepare your own review. You are very lucky as you have a choice. Make sure that you provide this choice to the person you support the next time the planning and review process is taking place.

Thinking activity

How would you feel if you were unable or not allowed to contribute to your own review process?

Practice activity 8

When preparing and writing your circle of relationships and one page profile how did you plan the process?

Was it important to have somebody there to help you?

Was carrying out this process helpful in making sure that you consider how you carry out further reviews with the person you support?

Section 5

Implementing person-centred thinking and person-centred reviews

Introduction

The final section of this guide explores how you and your team will implement person-centred thinking and person-centred reviews. You will need to know how to act on what is important to the person who you support and get to know how that person wishes to be supported. This includes knowing how to use person-centred thinking to respond to how different people communicate and overcome barriers to communication.

You need to be able to demonstrate how to empower someone to have maximum control and choice in their lives regardless of disability. A person-centred approach also means exploring how to support individuals in maintaining healthy relationships and being part of their community, and ensuring that they are always central to the person-centred review process. Finally, you will need to be able to make sure the planned outcomes from reviews actually happen.

Using person-centred thinking to know and act on what is important to the individual

Looking back to the person-centred values that we covered in the first section of this guide, a person-centred thinking tool needs to be used to act on what is most important to that individual. This process is not about what you want as a key worker, but what the person you are supporting finds most important to them. The person may have many different dreams and aspirations, some of which may sound ridiculous to you, but they are very important to them and should not be brushed aside because they seem too ambitious. Everyone has the right to dream and everyone has the right to express themselves in their own unique ways, as long as this does not hurt, harm or offend anyone else. When person-centred thinking and planning with a service user, it is important to give them time to express themselves and to be able to tell you exactly what is important to them. It is equally important to make sure that you report and record everything that they say so you can plan effectively with them. Person-centred thinking is about being flexible and responsive to the service user's needs and wishes. Make sure that you use the right person-centred thinking and planning tool in order to get the right outcome for them. This could be personal futures planning, essential lifestyle planning or a one page profile.

Establishing with the individual how they want to be supported

Always ensure that you find out exactly how an individual wants to be supported in the tasks and activities you are helping them to plan for. Knowing the support needs of the service user is really important so that they can be supported in the right way in the activities they want to participate in. It can be very easy to try and make decisions for the person you support and do things for them, because they may be slower than you at making decisions and acting on them. Try to resist taking decisions out of people's hands; give the people

Thinking activity

When preparing for a review with an individual that you work with, how do you make sure that you really understand what is important to that person?

It may help you to refer back to the one page profile and circle of relationships exercises in the previous section.

Key learning points

It is important to work with the person you support on what is important to them. Just because you do not feel that it is important, it does not mean that it is not.

You should offer the correct level of support to people – just enough but not too much.

that you work with a little more time to make decisions for themselves and by doing this you will give them complete ownership of the task. Equally, it is okay for an individual to fail at a task the first time they try to do it. It's okay not to get it right every time and you should not be perturbed by this. Life is all about making decisions and we all have the right to get things wrong. Make sure you use the planning and review process to explore these issues and then help the person to plan a different way. There is no excuse for not involving the individual in how they want to be supported. Even if they have a profound learning disability there are ways and means of helping them to be involved in making decisions, even if this is just a very small step. Find other people to help out, such as professionals from the multidisciplinary team, family members and friends, other team members who have known them for a long time, and advocates. Make sure that you are constantly supporting the individual to review the way they wish to be supported and that this is recorded in their person-centred plan.

Using person-centred thinking to know and respond to how the individual communicates

As we have previously explored, some people with a learning disability have quite limited communication. This can affect the way that they make decisions and their ability to make decisions and process information. The Mental Capacity Act (2005) explains more about how we should be exploring people's mental capacity when it comes to making decisions. If you

Thinking activity

Think about a time when you have supported someone in a task and you have had to establish the level of support they need.

Was anyone else involved in helping you eg. other professionals?

are working with a person with a profound and severe learning disability that affects the way they make decisions, then you should make sure that you are consulting with as many people as possible who have a vested interest in helping and supporting that person to live as full a life as possible. You should never isolate someone with severe learning disabilities and just assume that you are doing the best for them. It is important to make sure that you understand how an individual communicates and sometimes service users have little idiosyncrasies that only you or a few others may truly understand. Sometimes you know when a person means 'yes' and when they mean 'no', or when they are happy and when they are unhappy. It is important that you explore different ways of helping them to understand that it's okay to say 'I don't enjoy this' or 'I don't want to do this'. Also, you may know that certain individuals are vulnerable in certain situations and may express their vulnerability through behaviour that is inappropriate to the situation. It's really important that you work with them to empower them as much as is possible to be able to deal with all eventualities. Their behaviour in certain situations should not be a barrier to taking part in activities that they enjoy. Make sure that you always explore all help and options available to you to help the individual develop.

Key learning point

Get to know how the person communicates their feelings and try to encourage them to communicate them whenever they can, especially when they are doing something important like reviewing a plan.

Being responsive to how an individual makes decisions

Everyone makes decisions in different ways. Some of us are very proactive, making decisions on the spur of the moment; some of us like to consider all options and weigh up all the pros and cons. Being quick to act may make us an activist, thinking more about it may make us a reflector. Try and find out what sort of personality type the

Thinking activity

Consider a time when you wanted to tell someone something but could not. Perhaps you were nervous, ashamed, or just did not want to upset that person.

How did it make you feel?

What should you have done?

Practice activity 9

Write an account of a time when you had to help someone with a communication difficulty plan for their review.

How did you overcome the communication difficulty and successfully plan for the review, putting the individual at the centre of everything you did?

person you support is, by using the Honey and Mumford Personality Styles Test (1992). Understanding the way that they process information and the way that they make decisions may help you when supporting them. You should also try the Honey and Mumford test yourself – why not do it as an exercise in your next staff team meeting?

Thinking activity

How do you ensure that the person that you are supporting has maximum control and choice when implementing person-centred planning activities?

Whenever supporting someone to make decisions you should always ensure that you are not pushing them to arrive at a decision that they may regret. You should not rush them to make decisions and should always make sure that you present all information to them in a digestible format that they understand. This may involve the use of a communication system like Makaton or Widget.

However you present information, it should be appropriate to the person and allow them to have maximum choice and control in their own lives and decision-making. Remember, the decision is about them, and what they want to do and how they want to do it; your thoughts and feelings should not be part of this process. This applies equally to parents, families and friends, and other members of staff. The choice is theirs and not anyone else's.

Risk assessment is an important part of the person-centred thinking, planning and review process. When exploring different activities with the person that you work with, it is essential to make sure that all aspects of safety have been considered.

- A risk is defined as the likelihood of a hazard becoming a danger to the service user.
- A hazard is defined as something which has the ability to cause harm to the service user.

When planning any activity with a service user you should always identify any hazards that may become a genuine risk to that person. You need to think about how much damage the hazard could cause to the service user. You should then look at ways in which to minimise the risks that are caused by any hazards identified.

Risk assessments are all about making sure that the service user is as safe as possible at all times when carrying

Key learning point

Everyone makes decisions in different ways and we should always ensure that individuals make their own decisions for themselves, regardless of how they make them.

All the individual's relationships and special places need to be taken into consideration when reviewing their personal plan.

out activities of daily living. Risk assessments should never be used as an excuse to prevent service users from doing activities. They should be used in order to make the activity safer.

Supporting the individual in their relationships and in being part of their community

You may have to support someone in fostering relationships with the people that are closest to them. These may be their parents, their friends, their boyfriend, girlfriend, wife, husband or partner. There may be all sorts of complicated issues when it comes to supporting people in their relationships and it is important that you don't take any of these relationships for granted. These are relationships that belong to the person you are supporting, and not to you.

You may have to get involved in helping people to meet up or go on journeys with people that they are in relationships with. This may mean that you have to understand a little bit about the person that they have the relationship with and also what makes a relationship work, or in some cases, not work. You may find some relationships more difficult than others, for example parents who 'interfere too much', sexual relationships, and relationships where there is an argument or conflict. Although it is important that you do not interfere, it is equally important that you monitor the situation if you feel that these relationships are unhealthy for the individual you support and may be abusive. Relationships may be unhealthy and abusive on both sides – the person

Thinking activity

How do you ensure that these important people are incorporated into the review process and that this is appropriate for the individual that you work with?

you support may be the abuser. You should always seek advice and guidance from a senior member of staff if you are worried about any part of the individual's relationship. You should also make sure that you let them know about your concerns and that you will have to speak about them to a senior member of staff. In the end, you do have a duty of care under safeguarding vulnerable adults guidance (SOVA).

Thinking activity

What steps would you take to ensure that the individual who you support is at the centre of the review process?

You should also support the person you work with to participate in community activities if they want to. This includes visiting local community centres, using library facilities, going to pubs, restaurants and shops and any community groups and associations that they want to be involved with. As previously discussed, you should fully explore these activities with the individual and establish adequate risk assessments.

Ensuring that the individual is central to the person-centred review process

If you are following the steps that we have looked at in the sections of this guide, then you will be placing the individual at the centre of the person-centred review process. Person-centred planning should ensure that they are the driving force behind the planning process. They choose who they want to be involved in this process, whether it is family and friends or other members of staff. They should be valued within their community and we should ensure that their interests are always at the centre of everything that we do. They have the right to mutually satisfying relationships and we should always continue to listen, learn and plan with that person to help them get what they want out of life.

How to ensure that actions from a review happen

Finally, after doing all this work with the person you support throughout the person-centred planning and review process, you need to make sure that these actions actually happen. You should be chasing up actions with the relevant professionals, such as

Key learning point

The review process is all about the person that you support. They must inform the whole process and be at the centre of it.

It is important to follow up on all review items that do not happen and to report, record and find out why they are not happening.

psychologists, speech and language therapists, occupational therapists and general practitioners as necessary. Equally, do not be afraid to phone and write to the relevant social workers and case managers if you feel that actions are not happening. Make sure you keep written records and follow them up with the relevant people. Make an enquiry, or even a complaint, if actions are not happening. Do not be afraid to be pushy; you are working on the service user's behalf. (But there is a difference between being pushy, persistent and tenacious, and being rude!) Remember to keep the person you are supporting informed and involved as well.

Summary

This section should have reinforced the process of person-centred thinking, planning and review. You should be concentrating on how to involve people and make them your central focus when person-centred planning and reviewing their progress. You should be considering their communication needs, their support needs, what is important to them, and the relationships that they have and the part these play in their lives. Finally, it is important to remember that the planning and review process is a constant one and should be regularly updated. Actions should be followed up as a matter of course.

Thinking activity

Consider a time when you have had to follow up a difficult action from a review meeting.

Why was the action not happening and what did you do to try and make it happen?

Practice activity 10

From your experience of supporting a particular individual in reviewing their plan:

What did you do to make sure that the actions from a review actually happened?

Were there any actions which did not succeed?

What were the reasons for this?

Notes

Notes

Notes

Certificate of achievement

This is to certify that:

----

has achieved .... hours of study and work-based practice on supporting person-centred thinking and planning in learning disability by covering the following learning outcomes:

- *Understand the principles and practice of person-centred thinking, planning and reviews*
- *Understand the context within which person-centred thinking and planning takes place*
- *Understand own role in person-centred planning, thinking and reviews*
- *Be able to apply person-centred thinking in relation to own life*
- *Be able to implement person-centred thinking and person-centred reviews*

Signed: --

Title: --

References

Belbin M (2011) *Belbin Team Roles* [online]. Available at: www.belbin.com (accessed December 2012).

Department of Health (2001) *Valuing People: A new strategy for learning disability for the 21st century* [online] Available at: www.dh.gov.uk/en/publicationsandstatistics/publications/publicationspolicyandguidance/DH_4009153 (accessed December 2012).

Department of Health (2009) *Valuing People Now: A new three-year strategy for people with learning disabilities* [online]. Available at: www.dh.gov.uk/en/publicationsandstatistics/publications/publicationspolicyandguidance/DH_093377 (accessed December 2012).

General Social Care Council (2010) *Code of Practice for Social Care Workers.* London: GSCC.

Honey P & Mumford A (1992) *The Manual of Learning Styles* (3rd edition). Maidenhead: Peter Honey.

Pearpoint J, O'Brien J & Forest M (1993) *PATH: Planning possible positive futures.* Toronto: Inclusion Press.

Further reading

Brooke J (2007) *Principles of Learning Disability Support.* London: Heinemann/BILD.

Carnaby S (2011) *Learning Disability Today* (2nd edition). Brighton: Pavilion Publishing and Media Ltd.

Johnson D & Hardie E (2007) *Health and Safety in a Learning Disability Service.* London: Heinemann/BILD.

Pountney J (2007) *Protecting People who have a Learning Disability from Abuse.* London: Heinemann/BILD.

Pountney J (2007) *Your Role as a Learning Disability Worker.* London: Heinemann/BILD.